200 TIPS

for Growing

FLOWERS

in the

NORTHEAST

Miranda Smith

CHICAGO
REVIEW
PRESS

Library of Congress Cataloging-in
Publication Division

Smith, Miranda, 1944–
    200 tips for growing flowers in the Northeast /
Miranda Smith. — 1st ed.
        p.   cm.
    Includes Index
    ISBN 1-55652-251-7 (pbk.)
    1. Flower gardening—Northeastern States.
    I. Title.
SB405.5.N66S58   1996
635.9'0974—dc20   95-37096
                                              CIP

Published by Chicago Review Press, Incorporated
814 North Franklin Street
Chicago, Illinois 60610

ISBN 1-55652-251-7

5 4 3 2 1

CONTENTS

INTRODUCTION

This book is meant for both beginning gardeners and those with some experience. In it, I've tried to boil down the essentials of Northeastern flower gardening and concentrate them into easily understood tips that can guide you through the entire process—from planning and design, through cultural care and pest management, and on into cutting for the longest vase life.

The Northeast is a wonderful place to grow flowers. True, we can't grow tropical perennials in an outside garden, but there are a wealth of flowering plants we can grow, including some that couldn't look better in any other climate.

One of the most striking aspects of growing flowers in this region is the enormous variability in the climate. The old New England cliché, "If you don't like the weather, just wait ten minutes," holds for the entire Northeast. Not only do we have huge variations in the weather within the day, the week, and the month, we also have them from one year to the next. Some summers are so hot that you could easily think you'd traveled a hundred miles south without knowing it. Lovers of warm weather like zinnias and portulaca outdo themselves but the cool-lovers such as sweet alyssum are hard to coax into a second bloom. In other years, rain and constant cloud cover keep temperatures so cool you'd swear you were in northern Quebec. These are the seasons when the sweet alyssum and pansies steal the show but you have to remove the blossoms from soft-leaved plants to prevent them from rotting.

Northeasterners can count on some constant environmental factors too. No matter how "warm" a particular winter, for example, the ground will still freeze for a minimum of three months and a maximum of six. Our humidity levels, and our rainfall, are far higher than those in many areas of the country, even in what we consider a "dry" year. No matter if the spring comes early and the fall is late, our frost-free period is short enough so we have to transplant many of the long-season annuals. As well, some of our pests and diseases are so acclimated to the region that they're always with us, through the warm years and the cool ones, the dry ones and, most particularly, the soggy, wet ones.

So what's a Northeastern gardener to do? These tips are meant to answer that question. No matter whether you're in a colder-than-average horticultural zone 3 area or a protected spot in balmy zone 6, you'll find the techniques you need to keep your flowering plants growing well in our constantly fluctuating climate. You'll also learn about the growth habits and peculiarities of the flowering plants that do grow well in this region, sometimes described by the zones in which they thrive.

The "tips" format may make some readers think that this is a book about how to garden without doing any work. But that isn't so. Many labor-saving techniques, both for the short term and the long run, are presented and efficiency is stressed, but gardening, any kind of gardening, requires that you get out there and do it—plant the seed, keep it weeded, water it adequately, and protect it from pests and diseases. But that's as it should be. Once you learn how to garden in the Northeast, or anywhere else for that matter, you'll discover that the true joy of it doesn't come from the way the yard looks or the wealth of cut flowers you can have in every room. Instead, it's in the gardening itself—the "work" of it all. For most gardeners, this work is what makes the magic.

These tips are meant to help you through the rough spots of gardening in the Northeast so you'll love it too. Once you know how to protect your plants from diseases caused by our ever-present humidity levels, for example, or work with or modify a constantly wet soil, the characteristics of the Northeastern region can become advantages rather than frustrations.

Some tips are universal; they apply to all gardeners in all regions. Nonetheless, they are vitally important. Because they don't fit into the body of a book on growing flowers in the Northeast, I've saved them for the introduction. So without further ado, here are the first four tips to get you started on successful flower gardening in the Northeast.

Start small. Begin by planting a garden that you can easily maintain in a couple of hours on the weekend. As you outgrow it, add new sections gradually. This strategy allows you to grow into the work without regarding it as a chore or having weeds or pest problems build up.

Choose plants hardy to your zone. Whenever you're buying a perennial plant or choosing seed, check to see that the plant can grow in your horticultural zone. This simple precaution can save you endless aggravation and lots of sorrow since you won't even try to grow it if it's doomed to die over your long, cold winter season.

Spend gardening money wisely. Gardening can be very expensive, particularly when you develop a hankering for all the snazzy technologies available these days. So do yourself a favor and consider purchases carefully, buying only after you're sure it's not an impulse purchase that you'll later regret.

Enjoy yourself. This final unofficial tip is so simple it's easy to ignore. But please remember it. After you have the basics down, garden your own way. Hang convention. For example, if you feel like deviating from all the accepted design "rules" (many of which are presented here as tips), do it! Gardening isn't about impressing the neighbors anymore than it's a race or competition. You'll have to discover what it is about for you, but the only way to do that is to get out there and have a great time.

GROWING FLOWERS IN THE NORTHEAST

1 **Compensate for the cool, short Northeastern summer by buying transplants or starting seeds early, inside the house or in a greenhouse.** The abundant rainfall and moderate summer temperatures through the region are ideal for most flowering plants. But the frost-free season is short enough so that many annuals won't bloom until very late summer if they are seeded directly in the soil. Annual asters (*Callistephus chinensis*), bachelor's buttons (*Centaurea* spp.), impatiens (*Impatiens* spp.), lobelias (*Lobelia* spp.), marigolds (*Tagetes* spp.), petunias (*Petunia* x *hybrida*), pansies (*Viola* x *Wittrockiana*), and vincas (*Catharanthus roseus*) are among the annuals that should be transplanted so that you can enjoy them all through the summer.

◆2◆ Avoid disease problems caused by the high humidity levels in the Northeast by laying out your flower garden so that prevailing winds blow across the plants and leaving more room between plants than is sometimes recommended. These humidity levels are a mixed blessing. On the one hand, watering requirements are generally low because soils dry out slowly, but on the other, consistently high humidity makes your plants more susceptible to diseases, particularly those caused by fungi.

◆3◆ Concentrate on improving and maintaining your soil fertility and structure with two simple techniques–applying compost every year and testing for acidity every three years. Even though soil types vary so widely across the Northeastern region, ranging from thin, stony soils to dry, sandy ones to wet, dense clays, high acidity is almost always a given. Test your pH, or measure of acidity, and follow the testing lab's recommendations for applying ground limestone. As well, few Northeastern soils contain just the right balance of nutrients, the perfect mixture of particles, and the structure that allows for both good aeration and drainage. Compost improves all of these conditions.

4 **Take advantage of the low summer temperatures in the Northeast by planting flowers that thrive in coolness.** For example, even though pansies last no more than a few weeks in warmer climates, they'll bloom all season long in a Northeastern garden. As well, it's not uncommon for tulip and daffodil flowers to remain fresh for more than a week or for most perennials to bloom for a month rather than the listed 2 to 3 weeks. So whenever you curse the coolness of our climate, remember that your blooms last longer because of it.

What Every Flowering Plant Needs

5 **Please don't overfeed the daisies.** Flowering plants thrive with far lower quantities of nutrients, particularly nitrogen, than vegetable crops. As a general rule, annuals prosper in soil a little richer than that you would use for perennials but leaner than soil for vegetables. Most flowering plants profit from a yearly compost application. In the perennial bed, sprinkle about half an inch of compost onto the soil each spring and dig it in. For annuals such as pansies (*Viola* x *Wittrockiana*), zinnias (*Zinnia* spp.), and marigolds (*Tagetes* spp.), a half-inch is also appropriate, while for nasturtiums (*Tropaeolum* spp.), cosmos (*Cosmos* spp.), and portulaca (*Portulaca grandiflora*), it's best to plant in the lowest-fertility soils you have.

6 **Provide good soil drainage to keep your plants healthy.** Wet soggy soils promote root diseases and make perennial plants more vulnerable to winter damage. If your soil needs slight drainage improvement, yearly additions of an inch or two of finished compost may solve the problem. But really wet soils demand more serious corrective measures. To decrease early-season problems, dig drainage ditches to direct spring runoff away from the garden area. Raised beds—areas where you heap soil from the pathways into the beds—improve drainage all season.

7 **Correct the pH (acidity) of your soil to improve plant health and yields.** Soil acidity influences nutrient availability. For example, in high acidity soils, phosphorus tends to form tight chemical bonds with other soil elements. These molecules are resistant to being broken down, so no matter how much phosphorus is in the soil, it's absent from your plants' menu. Similarly, many essential trace nutrients aren't available in alkaline soils. Most flowers, like vegetables, grow best in soils that are slightly acid, 6.5 on the pH scale.

8 **Each time you're tempted to crowd just one more plant into a flower bed, consider whether you might be causing a potential disease problem.** Since high humidity is a given in the Northeast, err on the side of conservatism, especially while you're establishing a new garden bed. Rather than actually crowding the plants, create the illusion of fullness with plants such as baby's breath (*Gypsophila* spp.) that allow good air circulation while looking as if they are densely planted.

Dreaming Up Flower Gardens

◆ 9 ◆ Dream up a flower garden to suit your own particular tastes. Flower gardens are for the sheer enjoyment they give. Although all gardens can have as much to do with pleasure as they do with production, you'll never be able to justify a flower garden with high-sounding phrases about "growing your own" in the same way that you can rationalize an orchard, the herb garden, or vegetable beds. So go ahead—indulge yourself. And then, after dreaming about it, sit down to plan it carefully, taking account of sun and shade patterns in your yard, soil conditions in particular areas, and features such as slopes just begging for a rock garden.

◆ 10 ◆ If you want to create an old-fashioned cottage garden, concentrate on planting older varieties, especially those with strong fragrances. Check seed catalogues to locate plants such as single hollyhocks (*Alcea rosea*), fragrant sweet peas (*Lathyrus latifolius*), both annual and perennial scabiosa (*Scabiosa* spp.), delphiniums (*Delphinium* spp.), columbines (*Aquilegia* spp.), love-in-a-

6

mist (*Nigella* spp.), and old-fashioned roses (*Rosa* spp.). And don't forget to include the plants that bring back your sweetest flower memories.

11 **Flower gardens can evoke a mood as well as any song.** Take advantage of this by designing gardens that inspire the feelings you most enjoy. If you want to create a garden that cheers you up, concentrate on mixing bright-colored annuals such as sunflowers (*Helianthus* spp.) and zinnias (*Zinnia* spp.) with vivid lilies (*Lilium* spp.) and a riot of wild-colored dahlias (*Dahlia* spp.). Or, create a restful, quiet garden filled with shades of blue, white, and lavender, touched with accents of the softest pinks. Complete a quiet garden's mood by enclosing it with a sound-absorbing hedge of privet (*Ligustrum* spp.) or arborvitae (*Thuja* spp.). The rest of the world truly will go by this garden without your noticing.

12 **Take advantage of hot sunny areas with soils that dry quickly by planting the flowers that thrive in them.** Portulaca (*Portulaca grandiflora*), yarrow (*Achillea* spp.), tickseed (*Coreopsis* spp.), blanket flower (*Gaillardia* x *grandiflora*), sunflowers (*Helianthus* spp.), sea lavender (*Limonium latifolium*), coneflowers

(*Echinacea* spp.), and oriental and Iceland poppies (*Papaver* spp.) are among the plants that love these conditions.

<13> **Use shady spots to add some drama to your garden.** While conventional wisdom holds that few flowering plants can thrive in a shaded area, nothing could be further from the truth. Start the spring with flowering bulbs such as snowdrops (*Galanthus*) and glory-of-the-snow (*Chionodoxa*), add creeping phlox (*Phlox subulata*) and Jacob's ladder (*Polemonium reptans*) for a touch of early blue, and greet the summer with annuals and perennials that prefer some shade. Annual shade-lovers include: ageratum (*Ageratum houstonianum*), wax begonias (*Begonia semperflorens cultorum*), browallia (*Browallia* spp.), coleus (*Coleus hybridus*), Chinese forget-me-not (*Cynoglossum amabile*), bells of Ireland (*Moluccella laevis*), periwinkles (*Vinca minor*), pansies (*Viola* x *Wittrockiana*), and impatiens (*Impatiens* spp.). Perennials that prefer light shade include astilbe (*Astilbe* x *arendsii*), columbines (*Aquilegia* spp.), foxglove (*Digitalis* spp.), bleeding heart (*Dicentra* spp.), evening primrose (*Oenothera pilosella*), hosta lilies (*Hosta* spp.), true geraniums (*Geranium* spp.), balloon flowers (*Platycodon grandiflorus*), and windflower (*Anemone* spp.). Ferns and a

shade-loving ground cover such as sweet woodruff (*Asperula odorata*) can unite a composition of these plants, making your shady garden one of the nicest areas in the yard.

14 **Fortunately for gardeners with spots that don't drain well, some plants thrive with "wet feet."** Marsh marigold (*Caltha palustris*), marsh mallow (*Althaea officinalis*), sneezeweed (*Helenium autumnale*), cardinal flower (*Lobelia cardinalis*), astilbe (*Astilbe* x *arendsii*), yellow and blue flags (*Iris pseudacorus versicolor*), heartleaf bergenia (*Bergenia cordifolia*), beebalm (*Monarda* spp.), Japanese primrose (*Primula japonica*), and true forget-me-not (*Myosotis palustris*) are all wet-lovers. If you experiment with these plants, you're sure to find some that love the conditions.

15 **Foundation plantings don't have to be boring.** All too often, people stick with the expected and create a planting that looks no different than any other on the street. But you can be more creative. Try mixing the expected azaleas (*Rhododendron* spp.), yews (*Taxus cuspidata*), and junipers (*Juniperus* spp.) with interesting foliage plants such as artemisias (*Artemisia* spp.), hosta lilies (*Hosta* spp.), and lamb's ears (*Stachys lanata*). Or add a repeating color accent by bordering the planting with perennials and annuals of one or two colors that come into bloom at various times of the year. Tie this planting together, and separate it from the lawn, by mulching it with a thick layer of hardwood chips or bark mulch.

16 **Keep your perennial garden exciting by planning so you have blooms from late April to November.** As you list the plants you want to grow, note their bloom times. Ideally, you'll have new flowers opening just as the last ones are ready to be deadheaded. But don't be disappointed if you don't pull this off during the first year or two. For one thing, many perennials require a year or two to get large enough to bloom, so you're bound to have blank spots in the blooming calendar. Secondly, while catalogues and books can give you a fairly good idea of blooming season, environmental conditions in your garden may speed them up or slow them down.

Designing Flower Gardens

17 **No matter what your taste, formal or casual, your garden will be more beautiful if you design it before you begin planting.** Flower gardens come in all shapes and sizes. The traditional perennial border is generally longer than it is wide, although it has room for at least three or four tiers of plants across its width. Perennials usually form the mainstay of this bed, with a few annuals tucked in to carry color schemes or bloom through the season. Less formal garden shapes are more common these days, ranging from beds containing only a few plant species to those filled with a mixture of herbs, annuals, perennials, and even the odd vegetable or two.

18 **Design your cutting garden for practicality rather than appearance.** Though you can cut flowers from a decorative planting, a separate cutting garden allows you to cut to your heart's content without spoiling the look of the more formal flower beds. If possible, put cutting plants off to themselves behind a shed or other building. If your yard doesn't allow this sort of private spot, try planting them in a border around the vegetable patch or with the herbs at your back door.

19 **Most flowering plants look best when planted in odd-numbered groups.** If you look carefully at plans designed by landscape designers and experienced gardeners, you'll probably notice a strange similarity in design. When grouping small and medium-size plants, these designers usually place three of the same type together. Occasionally a plan will call for five of the same plant, but it's very rare that four, six, or eight are used. This design convention has arisen because odd groupings are more interesting to the eye than regular, predictable ones.

20 **Flower gardens with varying leaf textures are as interesting as those with a harmonious mixture of flower colors and forms.** Fortunately, it isn't difficult to plan a garden with both interesting leaves and a pleasing color scheme. Always imagine that you are standing well back from the garden when you are planning. In your mind's eye, visualize the combinations of leaf forms and colors, without their blooms, as you select plants and placements. For example, you might mass a group of broad smooth bergenia leaves in front of the spikes of bearded iris, or group some lacy columbines to one side of gracefully drooping daylilies.

21 **Differing heights are important to the composition of your flower beds and borders.** It's easy to succumb to the temptation to simply place the tallest plants at the back of the garden, the midsize ones in the middle, and the shortest in the front. This sort of plan does guarantee that all the plants are visible. However, it isn't as pleasing to the eye as a garden with surprising spikes in areas other than the back. For example, plant several delphinium somewhere in the middle of the garden. They'll bloom only a few weeks each spring and sometimes, again in fall. For the rest of the year, their midsize foliage happily blends into other leaves at that layer of the garden.

22 **When designing, remember that most flower beds do not have distinct "fronts" and "backs."** Certainly, those in front of a wall or at the back of the yard do, but most are visible from a number of different vantage points. So think of the center as the "back," placing your tallest, most dramatic plants here. Gently move down an imaginary slope from the center, placing midsize plants in the middle of the bed and smaller ones at the edges. In this case, you won't want to interrupt the mid-zone with many tall plants, since the plants on the other side of the bed are already providing unexpected visual interest.

23 **Flower beds and borders look best when the plants are tied together into a pleasing whole rather than when they seem more like an interesting collection of plants.** One of the easiest and most effective ways to unify a design is by choosing a plant or two to use as a repeating theme. For example, you might have a long border planting on one side of your yard that contains everything from pink peonies (*Paeonia* spp.) to silvery-blue globe thistles (*Echinops bannaticus*). By placing a group of long-blooming shasta daisies (*Chrysanthemum* x *superbum*) or clumps of delicate gray-leafed artemisias (*Artemisia* spp.) at irregular intervals down the border, you'll create unity within the planting.

24 **Repeating colors unify a garden as effectively as repeating plants.** But using this design technique is somewhat more difficult than repeating plants because there are so few flowers that are actually the same color. White blooms, for example, usually have undertones of pink, green, or yellow, while red blooms are generally more orange or more blue than clear red. Fortunately, you can reconcile different hues of the same color and make them appear more similar to each other. Separate them with wide swaths of green, silver, and gray foliage. Don't repeat the same white flowering plants near the plants you're using as a repeating color since white can make the differences more clear.

25 One-color gardens are never truly one color, but they can be magnificent. Of all the colors from which you can choose for a one-color theme, red is the most difficult. Warm reds fight with cool reds, for one thing, and certain hues of orange-reds make pink-reds look dingy and worn. So be careful if it's a red garden you want. On the other hand, with enough green and gray foliage, harmonious white, yellow, or blue gardens are all easy to achieve.

26 Plan mixed-color flower gardens as carefully as you do one-color beds. Though it may seem that you can get away with any combination in a bed like this, some are more pleasing than others. Try to keep color values similar. For example, if most of the flowers are pastels and subtle shades of cool blues and reds, a bright, orange 'Enchantment' lily will either be the only thing observers see or will deaden all the other colors.

27 **If your carefully planned flower bed has times when nothing is in bloom, take an informal tour of other gardens in the area.** Before long, you're bound to see some blooming plants that would fit nicely into your yard. Chances are that you can identify these plants with an illustrated book or even a nursery or seed catalogue. But if you can't identify the plant, you might try asking the owner. Most gardeners are more than happy to talk about their plants, especially when you're admiring them.

Planning Garden Layouts

28 **Graph paper is the best tool when planning the layout of your garden.** Let each square represent 6 or 12 square inches, taping sheets together if necessary. As you plan, note size, bloom time, and color of each grouping. By the time you finish, you should have a good idea of the relative "weight" of all the groupings you plan to combine.

29 Spacing flowering plants is not as straightforward as spacing herbs or vegetables. As well, few catalogues give you information about spacing requirements. If you know how large in diameter the mature plant grows, you can plan to leave that much space plus several inches for "breathing room." In cases where you haven't a clue about the final size, be conservative and leave at least 1 square foot for annuals and 2 square feet for perennials. If this spacing makes the garden look too spare, fill it in with small blooming annuals such as sweet alyssum (*Lobularia maritima*) that can be pulled if they begin to crowd the planting.

30 Use annuals to keep the perennial bed lively all season. If your perennial bed is in danger of having some gaps in the bloom calendar, look for annuals that can fill in. While purists tend to phase annuals out of perennial borders after the first few years, many gardeners have discovered that their qualities are too important to be ignored.

31 Plan to camouflage the old foliage of tulips, daffodils, and other spring flowering bulbs. If you remove the leaves before they've naturally browned and died down, your plants won't produce well the following spring. But you don't have to look at them while they yellow and wither. Instead, plant quickly growing annuals or an ornamental grass in their bed. By the time they look unattractive, you won't even notice them.

32 **Make your gardening chores easier by growing plants with similar environmental requirements in the same bed or small garden.** For example, if all the high water-users are located at one end of a bed, it will be an easy matter to see that this area gets twice the irrigation time as other places in the yard.

From Grasses to Gardens

33 **When you are transforming an old lawn into a garden, plan your strategy based on the time, energy, and materials you have available.** If you just till up the area and plant your flowers, you'll regret it for years to come. Many of the grasses in the lawn are likely to be perennial and spread by runners, so you'll be pulling them out of the flower bed for years. If you have the time and the materials to pull the grasses that come up near your plants and keep deep mulches on the balance of the soil, tilling and planting may be the right way to proceed. But think about it before committing yourself to this kind of work.

◆34◆ For the fastest results, remove the sod before you plant. Sod is a dense layer of roots that extends 4 to 6 inches into the soil. You can remove this layer by cutting through it with a sharp spade and then literally rolling and "peeling" it from the soil surface, using the spade to cut under it where necessary. Add copious (2 to 3 inches thick) amounts of compost to the underlying soil before you plant in this garden. And begin a new compost pile with the sod you removed from the area. Pile it up, laying it so that the grass faces the bottom of the pile and the layers of soil and roots face upward, and let it sit undisturbed for a few weeks. Then turn it as you do any other compost pile. By the following year, it will be a valuable source of nutrition for your plants.

◆35◆ Mulch your future garden to kill the sod. If you choose this method, begin the spring before you plant. As soon as the snow melts, cover your future garden with about half an inch of newspaper, overlapping the edges. Water this well. Cover the newspaper with several inches of straw to make it look more attractive. This mulching system prevents light from penetrating to the grass below without obstructing moisture and air movement, so the soil doesn't suffer. By the following spring, the grass roots will have died and earthworms, who love newspaper, will have turned most of the mulch into lovely humus.

36 **Eliminate grasses that spread by underground stems, or runners, by cover cropping.** Remove the sod layer in the spring and till. Just after the frost-free date, plant buckwheat. It will flower in midsummer. Let it bloom for several weeks and then pull it or till it into the soil. If the timing is correct, you'll get a second buckwheat planting from the seeds of the first. In September, till this buckwheat into the soil and plant winter rye a week afterward. The rye will grow during the fall and early the next spring. Till in the rye as soon as the spring soil is dry enough to work. Wait two weeks before planting your garden. As the rye decomposes, it releases compounds that are poisonous to grass roots and most annual weed seeds, so your new garden will be easy to weed.

37 **When you are developing a new garden area, consider building raised beds.** In the Northeast, raised beds can solve many of the most common problems. They promote good drainage and aeration, warm quickly in the spring, and are easily penetrated by plant roots. As well, since their location stays permanent, you can conserve compost and other soil amendments by adding them only where they're needed. You can separate raised beds from the rest of the yard by enclosing them with boards, old railroad ties, or materials such as clay tiles.

38 **To build a raised bed, first loosen the soil with a tiller or spading fork.** If you plan to enclose the bed, dig a trench so you can partially bury the boards or tiles. Anchor the enclosing material with small stakes, pounded into the soil on the outsides of each corner. If the soil in the bed is not deep enough, add purchased bags of topsoil or dig it from another part of the garden. Spread a layer of compost over the topsoil and work it into the top few inches. Let the bed settle for a week or so before planting in it.

FIRST THINGS FIRST

Soil Health

39 **Pay as much attention to the soil in your flower beds as you do to that in your vegetable garden.** Even though your flowers don't need the same high nitrogen levels that many vegetables require, they benefit as greatly from good soil texture, structure, drainage, and the presence of a diverse and high population of microorganisms and soil animals. The healthier they are, the more they resist pest and disease attack.

40 **The best gardening soils**

- hold moisture well but drain quickly enough so roots have adequate oxygen.

- have a loose, crumbly texture that roots can easily penetrate.

- have adequate and balanced nutrient supplies.

- are slightly acid (6.5 on the pH scale).

- have large numbers of many different types of soil life including microorganisms and soil animals.

41 **Develop respect for all the creepy, crawly, visible and invisible creatures in your soil.** After all, the microorganisms and soil animals create the best qualities of garden soils. They transform unavailable nutrients into forms plants can use, they exude secretions that "glue" the soil together in a crumb structure that allows it to hold both water and air, and they prey on many of the pest and disease organisms that can plague your plants.

42 **Feed the soil animals and microorganisms that keep your plants healthy.** In a vegetable garden, you can plant a crop each year for no other purpose than killing it and turning it back into the soil as a supply of new organic matter. But flower beds planted to perennial crops don't lend themselves to this technique. Instead, keep the supply of organic matter high by adding compost each year and mulching with materials such as straw, shredded leaves, or wood chips.

43 **Soil tests are always worth the effort.** They don't always tell you how much of each nutrient your plants will actually pick up from the soil, but they will tell you if there's a nutrient imbalance or if the soil needs lime. Take soil samples every three years, always in the same season. While spring might seem like the perfect time, you're likely to get more accurate results if you wait to sample until late summer.

44 **Correct the pH (acidity) of your soil to improve plant health and yields.** Soil acidity affects the health of your plants by influencing how much of each nutrient is actually available to the plants. For example, in highly acid soils, phosphorus tends to form tight chemical bonds with other soil elements. These molecules are resistant to being broken down, so no matter how much phosphorus is in the soil, it's absent from your plants' menu.

Correcting the pH usually makes all your plants healthier.

◆45◆ Check your soil test results for the content of usable phosphorus, potassium, and calcium. If the test comes back reading "Low" or "Very Low" in any of the above elements, your flowers will suffer if you don't amend the soil. Apply compost and then add another amendment that is high in the deficient element.

◆46◆ Use rock powders to add needed minerals to your soil. These materials release their nutrients slowly, so they are long-lasting and more gentle to your plants than synthetic fertilizers. Rock phosphate contains phosphorus, greensand contains potassium, and lagbenite (or Sul-Po-Mag) contains sulfur, potassium, and magnesium. Calcitic limestone is high in calcium while dolomitic limestone contains magnesium as well. Other rock powders such as granite dust and ground basalt contain valuable trace elements.

◆47◆ Bonemeal, containing high percentages of both calcium and phosphorus, is one of the best fertilizers for flower gardens. Though many people consider it too expensive for anything but tomato plants in the vegetable garden, it's worth its weight in gold for flowers. Routinely add a quarter cup of bonemeal to each planting hole for bulbs and work a light sprinkling of it into the soil around established perennials each spring.

48 **Extra nitrogen is as damaging to your plants as too little would be.** The first symptom of excess nitrogen is soft, "sappy" growth–leaves that are too green and soft and stems that bend too easily with long spaces between leaves or branches. Flowering is generally reduced and the colors are washed out. High populations of aphids and other sucking insects are another indication of excess nitrogen, as is a high incidence of fungus diseases. Avoid these problems by steering completely away from synthetic fertilizers containing nitrogen and by applying no more than half an inch of compost or aged manure to flower beds each year.

49 **If you have a supply of fresh manure, add it to the compost pile rather than the garden.** Fairly fresh manure contains high levels of nitrogen and other nutrients that can runoff with rainwater, contributing to the pollution of nearby lakes and streams.

However, once the manure is composted, the nutrients are held in place and no longer pose this threat.

50 **Compost manures at temperatures of 160°F or above to kill weed seeds.** Manure is chock-full of nutrients and beneficial organisms. However, it's also full of weed seeds that pass, unharmed, through the cow's digestive tract. If you add uncomposted manure to the garden, you'll be adding lots of weed seeds too.

Compost

51 **Learn to compost like the pros–microorganisms and soil animals.** But to do so, you'll have to rely on them. Composting is the process in which microorganisms decompose organic matter, changing it into humus-rich material. In the natural world, composting goes on all the time as flowers, leaves, and fruit drop to the ground and decay. Not only are these plants returning the nutrients they took from the soil while they were growing, they are adding compounds they manufactured from carbon dioxide in the air and hydrogen and water from the soil.

52 **Add humus to your soils to make them more like the ideal.** Humus is filled with nutrients, many of which are immediately available to your plants. Other compounds are not yet broken down into available nutrients but instead remain in reserve for microbial attack and transformation. Eventually, the humus becomes stable, meaning that it contains very few compounds that can be broken down. Even after humus has stopped being a nutrient source, it's a valuable component in your soils because it aids good structure and moisture and air retention.

53 **Make composts with three times the volume of dry materials as fresh, green ones.** Composting microorganisms require about 25 times more carbon than nitrogen in their diets. But you don't need to learn how much carbon or nitrogen all your composting ingredients contain. Just remember that dry weeds and stalks have high carbon levels while green material such as grass clippings are high in nitrogen. Kitchen scraps, excluding meat, usually have about 25 times as much carbon as nitrogen, but are so wet that you'll want to add them to other ingredients in a pile. Don't add any meat or grease to the compost pile because these ingredients attract dogs and cats.

54 **Build compost piles in layers for the best results.** Put a 6-inch layer of dry stalks on the bottom, cover it with a 2-inch layer of green material such as weeds, sprinkle a handful of any rock powder but lime on it, and add an inch or so of kitchen scraps. And then begin again with the 6-inch layer of dry material. If you have manure, you can add it as part of the green material layer. A sprinkling of good soil adds microorganisms. You can also buy compost activators, mixtures of beneficial decomposing microorganisms, to add to the pile, sprinkling them between the dry and green layers. Water the layers as you build so that light glints off the surfaces. After the pile is about 3 feet high, cover it with a tarp to keep the rain from saturating it.

55 **Watch your compost pile carefully for the first week after building it so you can make any needed adjustments quickly.** Well-made composts heat up to about 160°F in the center within 4 to 5 days and do not have an objectionable odor. But problems can happen. If your pile smells bad, it's probably wetter than the ideal—try to keep it about as damp as a squeezed-out sponge. If the pile is just a little too wet, use a garden fork to turn the pile upside down and inside out. When you turn it, you'll be drying it out a little by adding more air. But if it's soggy wet, a simple turning won't fix the problem. You'll have to add more dry material as you turn it. Compost piles that don't heat adequately are also common. They're usually too dry or too low in nitrogen. To add moisture, sprinkle as you turn the pile, making certain that all surfaces shine. To add nitrogen, mix in some grass clippings or a cup or two of bloodmeal as you turn it.

56 Use compost bins to make turning the piles neat and easy.
A set of three bins, side by side, allows you to build a pile in the first bin and then turn it into the second a couple of weeks later. Build a new pile in the bin you just emptied. In several more weeks, you turn the pile in the second bin into the third bin, turn the pile in the first bin into the second one, and build a new pile in bin number one. When you re-move the pile from the third bin, set it beside your container and cover it with a tarp because chances are that it needs to "finish" composting for a few weeks. Wait to use it until earthworms move into it and it does not heat after being turned.

57 If you're on a tight schedule, try "sheet composting." Rather than saving all your household scraps to add to a compost pile, dig them into the garden. To do this well, you must have a deep straw or rotted hay mulch spread over an area where plants aren't presently growing. Each day, take out your scraps and lift the mulch from a portion of the area. Dig a shallow trench, add the scraps, sprinkle soil over them, and replace the mulch. Keep moving along the area so scraps don't build up in any one spot. By the next spring, you'll have a very fertile area where your scraps have decomposed.

58 If the thought of turning a compost pile makes you love the landfill, try making a slow compost. Build the pile as suggested and then, rather than turning it, just stick the garden fork into it every few days and lift upwards to let some new air in. You can also buy a compost aerator tool—a long handle with a spring-loaded "turner" at the bottom that stays shut when you push it into the pile but opens when you withdraw it, letting air in. Slow composts aren't finished as quickly and may not have quite the same nutritional content as piles that are turned frequently, but they're still valuable amendments for your garden.

59 For the best and fastest composting results, turn your piles so that the inside material is moved to the outside and the outside material is moved to the inside. Turning speeds the process by adding the oxygen that microorganisms need to stay active. As well, by reversing the position of the materials, you're ensuring that all the ingredients are exposed to the high temperatures in the center that kill weed seeds and disease organisms.

60 If you're looking for a fast, efficient, and easy way to compost kitchen wastes, try a worm bin. Make one by filling a large plastic bin, about the size of a busboy's tub, with a good soil mix to which you've added 5 to10 percent of autumn leaves and a sprinkling of bonemeal. Again, the material should be about as moist as a squeezed-out sponge. Now add about a pound of red wriggler worms (check the back of gardening magazines for suppliers). Each day, use a blender or the steel knife on the food processor to chew up kitchen scraps (no meat) and sprinkle it in an "H" pattern on the top of the soil surface. Cover the box with moistened, but not soggy, newspapers. Within only a few months, your worms will have transformed the garbage into the richest fertilizer of all—worm castings.

61 **Let your compost "mature" be-fore using it in potting soils.** Immature compost often contains chemical compounds that can be injurious to plants. You'll know your compost is finished when it looks and smells like good soil and no longer heats after being turned. At this point, you can add it to the garden soil without worrying. But if you want to mix it into a medium for containers, let it mature, covered by a rainproof tarp or in a covered barrel, for 1 to 3 months. All this time, a very slow decomposition process is transforming it into a much more stable form of humus.

PLANTING YOUR GARDEN

❀ ❀ ❀

Starting Seeds

62 **Starting plants from seeds completely changes your gardening budget.** For example, buying ten or fifteen astilbe plants from a nursery could cost you anywhere from $50 to $120. But a seed packet will only cost $2 or $3 and will usually provide 40 to 45 plants.

63 **Starting your own seed allows you to choose the most appropriate plants and varieties for your garden.** Garden centers grow and sell the most popular plants, never the unusual. Each winter, thumb through a variety of seed catalogues, looking for plants to complement your design. Try to resist the temptation to buy more than you need, but if you do, save the packets for another year.

64 **Make a chart to schedule sowing dates for each plant you're growing.** For plants that must be started inside, use information in the seed catalogue to learn when you should plant them. Cold-hardy perennials are planted about 8 to 10 weeks before the frost-free date, for example, while most tender annuals are started about 6 weeks before that date.

65 **Plant quickly flowering annuals several times during the spring and early summer to keep a steady supply of fresh bloom.** Sweet alyssum (*Lobularia maritima*), nemophila (*Nemophila menziesii*), and annual baby's breath (*Gypsophila elegans*), for example, flower in only 9 or 10 weeks from the sowing date but have a short bloom period. If you transplant seedlings in the spring and direct-seed new plants in late May and again in mid-June, you'll be able to enjoy them until frost.

66 Start most hardy annuals in side, about 8 to 9 weeks before the frost-free date. This schedule allows you to transplant sturdy seedlings a couple of weeks before the frost-free date. Use this schedule when starting the following plants: sweet alyssum (*Lobularia maritima*), calendula (*Calendula officinalis*), carnation (*Dianthus caryophyllus*), love-in-a-mist (*Nigella* spp.), pansy (*Viola* x *Wittrockiana*), phlox (*Phlox* spp.), poppy (*Papaver* spp.), painted tongue (*Salpiglossis sinuata*), snapdragon (*Antirrhinum majus*), statice (*Limonium sinuatum*), and sweet pea (*Lathyrus latifolius*).

67 Wait until about 6 weeks before the frost-free date to start the quickly growing tender annuals. Among these are: ageratum (*Ageratum houstonianum*), aster (*Callistephus chinensis*), bachelor's buttons (*Centaurea* spp.), Swan River daisy (*Brachycome iberidifolia*), browallia (*Browallia* spp.), celosia (*Celosia cristata*), cosmos (*Cosmos* spp.), dahlia (*Dahlia* spp.), gazania (*Gazania linearis*), hibiscus (*Hibiscus* spp.), marigold (*Tagetes* spp.), nicotiana (*Nicotiana* spp.), petunia (*Petunia* x *hybrida*), salvia (*Salvia* spp.), pincushion flower (*Scabiosa atropurpurea*), sunflower (*Helianthus* spp.), and zinnia (*Zinnia* spp.).

68 Use peat or paper pots to start plants with sensitive roots. Some plants die or bloom too early (and too sparingly) if their roots are disturbed during transplanting. Pots that you can bury with the seedling allow you to transplant these seedlings without damaging the roots. The following plants all appreciate this treatment: cleome (*Cleome hassleriana*), cosmos (*Cosmos* spp.), flowering cabbage, gazania (*Gazania linearis*), larkspur (*Consolida ambigua*), lupine (*Lupinus* spp.), nasturtium (*Tropaeolum* spp.), love-in-a-mist (*Nigella* spp.), poppies (*Papaver* spp.), sunflower (*Helianthus* spp.), and sweet peas (*Lathyrus latifolius*).

69 Plant disease-prone seeds such as vinca (***Catharanthus roseus***) and phlox (***Phlox* spp.**) in a sterile mix to prevent rotting diseases. Use a half-and-half mixture of milled sphagnum peat moss and fine horticultural vermiculite to make this media. Because it doesn't contain nutrients, you'll need to transplant your seedlings to a mix containing compost as soon as the first true leaves develop.

70 Use a soil mix that contains compost for starting most flower plants. The compost will give them the nutrients they need for a good start as well as protect them against some diseases. Make this soil mix from one-third compost, one-third milled sphagnum peat moss, one-sixth vermiculite, and one-sixth perlite or washed sand. This mix will sustain the plants for 6 to 8 weeks. By then, most plants are big enough to transplant.

71 **To avoid crowding in seedling flats, plant seeds at least half an inch apart.** If you have trouble seeding precisely, try the following tricks. Place medium-size seeds—the size of love-in-a-mist (*Nigella* spp.) or larkspur (*Consolida ambigua*)—on a small saucer and use the moistened tip of a wooden chopstick to pick them up. You can handle them one by one with this method. When planting seeds that look like nothing more than dust, petunia (*Petunia* x *hybrida*) and snapdragon (*Antirrhinum majus*) for example, add fine vermiculite to them. Then form a furrow in the flat and lightly sprinkle the vermiculite/seed mixture into it.

72 **Give "winter" to those seeds that can't germinate without it.** Some of these seeds require a period of freezing while others break dormancy when exposed to temperatures of 35 to 50°F for a specific length of time. This process, known as stratification, is easy to accomplish with a freezer and a refrigerator. The following chart gives temperatures and durations for common flowers that require this treatment.

Asters, perennial (*Aster* spp.)
  40°F   7 Days

Bells of Ireland (*Moluccella laevis*)
  50°F   5 Days

Carnation (*Dianthus caryophyllus*)
  Freeze   7 Days

Bachelor's Button (*Centaurea* spp.)
  40°F   5 Days

Columbine (*Aquilegia* spp.)
  40°F   5 Days

Pinks (*Dianthus* spp.)
  Freeze   14 Days

Delphinium (*Delphinium* spp.)
  Freeze   24 Hours

Purple coneflower (*Echinacea purpurea*)
  40°F   5 Days

Black-eyed Susan (*Rudbeckia* spp.)
  40°F   5 Days

Lupine (*Lupinus* spp.)
  Freeze   24 Hours

Maltese cross (*Lychnis chalcedonica*)
  35–40°F   5 Days

Pansy (*Viola* x *Wittrockiana*)
  40°F   24 Hours

Phlox, perennial (*Phlox* spp.)
Freeze   40 Days

Primrose (*Primula* spp.)
35–40°F   48 Hours

Snapdragon (*Antirrhinum majus*)
Freeze   48 Hours

73 **Use a cold frame to stratify seeds that require freezing before they will germinate.** In the late fall, plant the seeds in a deep flat or pot. Place the flat in a cold frame you can prop open on sunny days and remember to water until the medium is completely frozen. In December, when light is low and nighttime temperatures are reliably cold, you can close the cold frame for the winter. If you get a midwinter thaw, vent the frame when interior temperatures hit 75°F. Check moisture levels too. The seeds will germinate in early spring, long before they would have in the garden.

74 **You can also stratify seeds in the garden, right where they'll grow the following year.** Again, wait until late fall and then scatter tiny, frost-requiring seeds such as poppies (*Papaver* spp.) or pansies (*Viola* x *Wittrockiana*) on the soil surface. Plant larger seeds, such as bachelor's buttons (*Centaurea* spp.) and delphiniums (*Del-*

phinium spp.), at their normal depth. Once the ground has frozen, mulch the area well. In spring, draw back the mulch once the snow has melted and wait for your seeds to germinate. Thin or transplant seedlings if you seeded thickly.

75 **If directions call for "scarifying" seeds, pass them over fine sandpaper or lightly nick them with a sharp paring knife.** This damages a tough seed coat enough so that the developing root and seed leaves can emerge from it. (Remember the distinction between stratification and scarification by associating the latter with being "scared" to have your seed coat damaged.) After scarifying, soak seeds in water for 24 to 48 hours before planting. In nature, the seeds that require this treatment go through birds' digestive systems, where acids soften the seed coat. Scarify morning glory (*Ipomoea* spp.) and hibiscus (*Hibiscus* spp.) as well as seeds for shrubs that produce berries.

76 **Soaking seeds for 8 to 48 hours speeds germination and increases rates.** This technique is practical for large seeds. Tiny seeds are too hard to handle once they're wet. If the seed packet does not specify the length of time that a seed should be soaked, don't leave it in the water more than 24 hours. When directions ask that you soak for longer than this, remember to change the water every day during the soaking time. Lupine (*Lupinus* spp.), morning glory (*Ipomoea* spp.), nasturtium (*Tropaeolum* spp.), and sweet pea (*Lathyrus latifolius*) all respond well to soaking.

77 **If a seed is tiny, suspect that it requires light to germinate.** Simply press these seeds into the soil mix. To keep them sufficiently wet, cover the top of the starting container with a sheet of plastic wrap. If the flat is in a south-facing window where the sun can heat the soil mix to temperatures of 85°F or above, pull back the plastic wrap during the daytime to let excess heat escape. The following seeds require light to germinate: ageratum (*Ageratum houstonianum*), sweet alyssum (*Lobularia maritima*), columbine (*Aquilegia* spp.), artemisia (*Artemisia* spp.), begonia (*Begonia* spp.), chrysanthemum (*Chrysanthemum* spp.), coleus (*Coleus hybridus*), tickseed (*Coreopsis* spp.), foxglove (*Digitalis* spp.), dusty miller (*Centaurea cineraria*), coral bells (*Heuchera* spp.), impatiens (*Impatiens* spp.), lobelia (*Lobelia* spp.), nicotiana (*Nicotiana* spp.), petunia (*Petunia* x *hybrida*), balloon flower (*Platycodon* *grandiflorus*), portulaca (*Portulaca grandiflora*), primrose (*Primula* spp.), and snapdragon (*Antirrhinum majus*).

⟨78⟩ Darkness aids germination for some flower seeds. To achieve this, cover the starting flat with plastic wrap to retain moisture and then set a thick layer of newspaper over it. Although black plastic may seem appropriate, it usually overheats the medium. Peek under the newspaper every day and remove all coverings when the first seed germinates. Dark germinators include thrift (*Armeria pseudarmeria*), black-eyed Susan (*Rudbeckia* spp.), purple coneflower (*Echinacea purpurea*), calendula (*Calendula officinalis*), nemesia (*Nemesia strumosa*), primrose (*Oenothera* spp.), globe amaranth (*Gomphrena globosa*), statice (*Limonium* spp.), verbena (*Verbena* spp.), and vinca (*Catharanthus roseus*).

⟨79⟩ Transplant seedlings in a starting flat before they become crowded. This process, called "pricking out," is a delicate undertaking. Wait until the first true leaves–the pair that follow the seed leaves–enlarge before transplanting them. Then gently remove the soil mix, without touching the plants, and set it on a dampened towel.

Now separate the plants, a few at a time, and plant them in a larger container. Don't hold them by the stems or true leaves. Try not to touch anything but the root mass in the soil mix, but if you must touch a leaf, make it a seed leaf. Keep the balance of the seedlings covered with the damp towel while you work so they don't dry out.

◇80◇ Give seedlings high light so they will develop into vigorous, healthy plants. Light on a windowsill is almost never adequate. You can supplement it by hanging 4-foot fluorescent fixtures from the ceiling, suspending them from a chain. Use one warm daylight and one cool daylight bulb in each fixture. Adjust the chains so that the bulbs are never farther than five inches from the tops of the plants.

◇81◇ Light duration is also important to seedlings. Most require a 12-hour photoperiod, so unless otherwise directed by the seed catalogue or package description, follow this regime. Save yourself worry by plugging the light fixture into a timer that turns the lights on and off. You'll get the best results by setting the lights to go on at about 6:00 A.M. and off at 6:00 P.M.

82 **Water seedling flats from the bottom.** This ensures that the soil is thoroughly moistened and also keeps seeds from moving too far from where you planted them. Fill a large, flat plastic container with 2 inches of water, set your flat in it, and leave it there until the soil surface glitters with moisture. In soil mixes with adequate amounts of peat moss, vermiculite, and perlite, this only takes a minute or two, so you can water quickly.

83 **Choose the correct container size for your seedlings.** Small annuals can be started in 2-inch pots or plastic inserts, but larger annuals and most perennials grow better in a 3- to 4-inch pot. Since you won't be planting huge numbers of them, it's worth the extra space to produce a healthier plant.

84 **Use soil-heating cables or plastic heating mats to keep the temperature of the seed-starting medium warm enough for good germination.** But move the plants as soon as they have sprouted since seedlings are always healthier when they grow in an environment about 10°F cooler than their ideal germination temperature. Temperatures in your house will be suitable for almost everything you grow, with the possible exception of cool-lovers such as snapdragons (*Antirrhinum majus*). If these plants begin getting too tall and spindly—and have adequate light—they're probably too warm. Move them to a cooler location, setting them under artificial lights if necessary.

85 **Protect your seedlings from damping-off diseases by maintaining a good environment for them.** These diseases, caused by moisture-loving fungi, rot seeds as they germinate or soon after they emerge from the soil. To avoid them, keep the relative humidity low by watering only as necessary and use artificial lights to supply high light intensity for at least 12 hours of the day. Finally, keep a fan blowing in the room where they are growing. Good air circulation blows excess humidity away from the plants, preventing many of these fungi from germinating.

86 **"Harden off" seedlings before transplanting them to the garden.** Take them outside on a warm day about a week before you plan to transplant them. Put them in light shade and bring them inside that night. Each day, expose them to increasing amounts of light and wind. After about four days, begin leaving them outside all night.

Throughout this time, underwater them slightly–but not so much that they wilt. By the end of a week, they will be ready to face the rigors of the outside garden.

Transplanting

87 **Transplant hardy perennials and annuals up to three weeks before the frost-free date.** It's always safest to wait until after this date to transplant, but since you need to schedule your work time as carefully as the seedlings' starting time, move out the most cold-hardy plants before then. If a hard frost is predicted after you've got them planted, cover the plants as carefully as you do tomatoes in September. Hardy plants include sweet alyssum (*Lobularia maritima*), asters (*Aster* spp.), baby's breath (*Gypsophila* spp.), candytuft (*Iberis* spp.), carnations (*Dianthus caryophyllus*), columbine (*Aquilegia* spp.), delphinium (*Delphinium* spp.), pinks (*Dianthus* spp.), dusty miller (*Centaurea cineraria*), larkspur (*Consolida ambigua*), lupine (*Lupinus* spp.), love-in-a-mist (*Nigella* spp.), pansy (*Viola* x *Wittrockiana*), poppy (*Papaver* spp.), purple coneflower (*Echinacea purpurea*), perennial scabiosa (*Scabiosa caucasica*), perennial statice (*Limonium* spp.), sweet pea (*Lathyrus latifolius*), thrift *(Armeria pseudarmeria*), veronica (*Veronica* spp.), and yarrow (*Achillea* spp).

88 **Try not to buy seedlings with blooming flowers.** Even though they give you an "instant" garden, it's rarely the best one. Plants that are transplanted "green," before they have flowered, have time to establish a good root system before they put energy into making flowers and seeds, so they are usually healthier. If you do buy flowering plants, try to make yourself pinch off the flowers and buds when you transplant them. After about a week to 10 days, the plant will be established enough to withstand flowering with no loss of vigor.

89 **Pay attention to the details when transplanting, and you'll always have success.**

- Pick a cool cloudy day for the job or wait until after 4:00 P.M.

- Be certain that the soil is only moderately moist—wet soils compact easily.

- Set the seedlings in several inches of water for 10 minutes to soak their root balls.

- Gently pat the soil around the transplanted seedling to put its roots in contact with the soil.

- Water after you finish the job and when the weather's hot and dry, every day until the seedling is established.

90 Give plants a nutritional boost in early spring when soil temperatures are below 50°F. This boost helps to get their root growth off to a healthy start. One of the easiest ways to supplement their nutrition is by adding a tablespoon of liquid seaweed and a tablespoon of fish emulsion to every gallon of water you use for soaking root balls. If the weather persists in being cold for a few weeks and plants are unnaturally yellowish or purplish, water with a seaweed/fish emulsion dilution or compost tea as well.

91 Handle peat pots with care when you're transplanting and they'll soon be one of your favorite starting containers. Because the peat from which they're made is so water-absorbent, any surfaces left above the soil surface can wick moisture away from the root ball. Avoid this by tearing off the tops and burying the remainder of the pot at least an inch deep. Other problems are caused by the toughness of the material. Since thin delicate roots have trouble growing through it, give them a hand by slitting the sides of each pot before you plant it.

92 You can usually rescue seedlings in a crowded starting flat. The trick is to do it without damaging their roots. Begin by thoroughly soaking the flat. After it's wet, run a table knife around the edges of the medium. Now turn the flat upside down, placing your fingers between seedling stems if possible. Shake gently. The medium—held together by a tangle of roots—usually falls out. Set it upright on a damp towel and begin to tease the seedlings apart. In worst-case scenarios, you may have to sacrifice a few plants in order to rescue the others.

Direct Seeding

93 Some annuals are so quick to flower that you can seed them directly in the garden and get good blooms, even in the short-season Northeastern climate. The best choices for direct seeding include calendula (*Calendula officinalis*), clarkia (*Clarkia amoena*), morning glory (*Ipomoea* spp.), cosmos (*Cosmos* spp.), annual blanket flower (*Gaillardia pulchella*), small-flowered marigolds (*Tagetes* spp.), nasturtium (*Tropaeolum* spp.), nemesia (*Nemesia strumosa*), pincushion flower (*Scabiosa atropurpurea*), sunflower (*Helianthus* spp.), and zinnia (*Zinnia* spp.).

◆ **94** ◆ **Keep seeds uniformly moist while they are germinating.** In hot weather, this can be a challenge, but these simple methods usually work. Begin by making a small, ½- to ¾-inch depression where you're planting. After laying your seed on the soil surface in this depression, cover it with no more than ¼ inch of vermiculite. Sprinkle the area thoroughly so that the vermiculite is completely moist. In most cases, a daily sprinkling will keep the moisture-holding vermiculite damp enough so that seeds won't dry. However, if you're having a drought, cover the area with damp newspaper or floating row-cover material as well. Peek underneath every day so that you can remove the cover as soon as sprouts appear.

◆ **95** ◆ **If you fall behind in your spring starting schedule, don't despair.** In the case of some annuals, you will have to wait until the following year to plant them. However, many perennials take well to being started in summer and transplanted into the garden in early fall. The following plants can all be started as late as early July in the Northeast: astilbe (*Astilbe* x *arendsii*), perennial asters (*Aster* spp.), bells of Ireland (*Moluccella laevis*), black-eyed Susan (*Rudbeckia* spp.), columbine (*Aquilegia* spp.), perennial dianthus (*Dianthus* spp.), forget-me-not

(*Myosotis palustris*), foxglove (*Digitalis* spp.), pansy (*Viola* x *Wittrockiana*), balloon flower (*Platycodon grandiflorus*), perennial statice (*Limonium* spp.), sweet William (*Dianthus barbatus*), and yarrow (*Achillea* spp.).

◆96◆ **When starting seedlings in midsummer for a fall transplanting, keep them growing strongly until you move them to the garden beds.** Start them in flats or small pots as usual, but transplant them into large containers before their roots begin to get crowded or encircle the perimeter of the pot. Choose a 4- to 6-inch pot for small plants such as pansies, but use 12-inch pots for the others. You'll have to dig a bigger transplant hole in the fall, but your plants will be better able to withstand the winter.

Artificial Supports

◆97◆ **Make trellises for climbing plants sturdy enough so they remain upright in high winds and heavy rains.** If you are building a trellis, make the bottom stakes so they extend at least a foot into the soil. After setting a trellis in place, push against it to see if you can budge it. If you can, add 9- or 10-gauge wires to the sides and secure them to the ground with foot-long metal stakes. Mark the stakes and wires so visitors or lawn mowers won't run into them.

98 **Give your garden some unexpected drama with a pillar trellis or two.** Make pillars from a wire fencing material formed of both horizontal and vertical wires. Bend the fencing into an appropriately-sized circle, anywhere from 3 to 6 feet in diameter. Cut through the vertical wires on one side and bend them into hooks that you can use to hold your circle together. Now cut through the horizontal wires on the bottom to make "stakes," at least 6 inches long, that will push into the soil. Further secure the pillar by pounding two or three wooden stakes into the soil on the inside of the pillar. Tie the pillar to the stakes. Plant two or three of the same climbers around the perimeter and train or tie them to the pillar as they grow.

99 **Make your own ring or hook supports for plants that droop.** Garden supply houses sell lovely green wire supports, but they cost enough so that many people forgo them. But don't let cost dissuade you; make your own from 9- or 10-gauge wire. Cut the wire with snips and bend it into the desired shapes with a pair of pliers. Once you have a roll of wire and some snips, you'll discover how much difference a little support can make.

◆100◆ Use inexpensive bamboo stakes to radically improve the appearance of plants such as lupines (*Lupinus* spp.) or delphiniums (*Delphinium* spp.) that form tall flower spikes. Lay in a good supply so that you can stick them into place as flower stalks begin to elongate. Use green twistee-ties to secure the flower spikes. Leave some slack in the twistee so that it won't injure the stem.

◆101◆ Use an arbor to highlight the pathway into the garden or support a heavy wisteria vine. You can purchase an arbor ready-made, or build your own. If you choose to build, remember that you should construct it from materials that are suitable for whatever plants you're growing on it. For example, wisteria (*Wisteria* spp.) or grape vines are so heavy that all the outside supports should be made of strong metal pipes or 4 x 4 wooden posts, while clematis (*Clematis* spp.) arbors can be made of thin wooden lathing secured to 2 x 3 or even 2 x 2 posts.

CARING FOR YOUR GARDEN

❀ ❀ ❀

Mulching

 A combination of newspaper and straw makes a mulch that few weed seedlings can penetrate. Begin by laying down a layer of newspaper over the areas you want to mulch. If you have lots of vigorous perennial weeds, such as quack grass or bindweed, make the newspaper layer an inch or so thick. However, if annual weeds are your bane, three or four sheets of newspaper will do the trick. Wet the newspaper thoroughly and then cover it with a layer of straw. The straw is as much for appearance's sake as utility, so your layer only needs to be deep enough to hide the newspaper. If you don't use straw, weight the newspaper mulch with rocks or boards to keep it from flying away in strong winds.

103 **Think twice before using rotted hay as a mulch.** It does add a great deal of carbon to feed microorganisms and soil animals, keeps the soil evenly moist, and discourages some pests. However, unlike straw, most hay contains numerous weed seeds. So if you use it, be prepared to keep adding layers to it, through the season as well as in following years, to mulch out the grasses and other weeds that it brings into your garden.

104 **Shred your autumn leaves before using them as a mulch.** Otherwise, all the flat ones—such as maples—will mat on the soil surface, preventing air and water movement. But you don't need an expensive shredder for this job. Instead, run a lawn mower through your leaf piles, several times in several directions. It won't take long before they're in small pieces.

105 Use shredded hardwood bark or wood chips to give your perennial beds a really "finished" look. These materials are so slow to break down that a thick layer will last for at least two years. After that, you may need to add thin layers every year or so. The high carbon content of bark and wood chips means that microorganisms will require soil nitrogen while they are slowly decomposing them. If the soil is rich, you won't need to add any fertilizer for a year or two. However, in lean soils, supplement fertility before you mulch and every spring afterward. Use a gallon of manure tea or a 50/50 mixture of liquid seaweed and fish emulsion, diluted as recommended on the bottle, for every square foot of growing area.

106 Landscape cloth is a boon in the flower garden. Weeds simply can't penetrate it, though water and air can. It takes many years to break down, so it's a long-term labor-saving device as well. Lay it over the area you want to mulch. To keep it in place, use U-shaped ground staples or bury the edges. Cut out circles or squares for transplants. Once the area is planted, cover the landscape cloth with straw or wood chips to make the area look its best.

107 Use ground covers around large woody perennials and bushes to keep weeding to a minimum. However, when you use them, be certain to keep the area well watered and fertilized so that your perennials do not suffer from the competition. As well, the perennials will be healthier if you leave about 12 inches of bare soil between their trunks or stems and the beginning of the ground cover planting. Expect to weed out the encroaching ground cover in early spring, midsummer, and early fall.

Watering

108 Time your watering well. To make the best use of your water supplies, water early in the morning, before the sun is high enough to encourage rapid evaporation. When you have to water later in the day, try to finish in time so that leaves dry before nightfall. Wet leaves invite attack by fungi that germinate in a film of water.

109 Pay attention to how your plants look when you're deciding whether or not to water. Most gardening books recommend that plants receive about an inch of water a week. But since requirements vary with both the weather and the species, that's only a guideline. Your plants are the best indicators. The minute leaves look a bit dull, well before they droop, stick a finger into the soil to check moisture levels. If the soil is dry, water. Remember too that an "inch of water" translates into 2 gallons per square foot of growing area.

110 **Consider a drip irrigation system if you want to conserve water or are away from home during good watering hours.** Even though these systems are expensive to install, they are usually very cost-effective over the long term. Most irrigation suppliers provide good directions for setting up the system so that individual plants in a growing bed have adequate water. Pay attention to these recommendations because the people who make them have learned from experience. And ask about timers if you are frequently away from home. This feature alone can pay back the cost of the system over a couple of years.

111 **For a less expensive water-conserving system, use soaker hoses.** These hoses are made of a semi-porous material that allows water to ooze from it, all down the length of the hose. Try using them under the mulch in shaded areas. Because they don't wet the leaves, they do as much for disease prevention as they do for watering convenience.

112 **Used well, a simple sprinkler can be one of the best irrigation methods going, particularly in the Northeast, where evaporation is slow in the cool early morning.** Sprinkle early in the day so that plants dry before dark and always check that the wind isn't interfering with the watering pattern you envisioned when you positioned the sprinkler. Even if you have a drip system, you'll want to keep a few sprinklers on hand for emergency watering.

Weeding

113 **If you don't want to mulch your flower garden, you'll have to weed.** Make a resolve to weed early and often. Young weeds are easy to kill, so you save time in the long run by weeding while they're small. As well, your plants will be healthiest and look their best if they are kept weed-free in the beginning of the year. Once your flowers begin to get large, they'll shade out any new weeds that appear.

◇114◇ **Some weeds are capable of re-rooting almost as fast as you pull them.** Whenever you're weeding purslane, small-seeded galinsoga, grasses, lambsquarters, or red-root amaranth, pile the weeds in a bucket or cart and remove them from the garden. Don't ever let these weeds sit on the pathway where you might step on them and inadvertently replant them.

◇115◇ **Cut down on your future weeding by preventing annual weeds from flowering.** These plants make thousands and thousands of seeds. So even if you don't have time to keep your garden totally weed-free, patrol daily, pulling weeds that are about to flower or pulling off the flower heads. Some weeds can ripen their seeds after the flower has been picked, so it's best to pick them into a bucket.

◇116◇ **Do your best to eliminate perennial weeds.** Walk the garden in the early spring, taking your spade with you. Dig out every weed you see, putting it into a bucket or cart for removal from the garden. In the case of weeds such as poison ivy, whose roots travel long distances under the soil, dig out as much as you can. In worst-case scenarios, you may have to cover these persistent perennials with a deep mulch for as long as a season.

117 **Before you make your yard a totally "weed-free" zone, plant some wildflowers on the borders and tuck small-flowered plants into flower beds.** Many of the beneficial insects that help to keep your pests under control are reliant, particularly in the adult phase of their lives, on the nectar and pollen that the weeds used to supply. As long as you supply replacement plants, your beneficial insects will never notice the disruption in their habitat.

Getting Rid of Insect Pests

118 **Building the soil health and growing many different plants are two of the most important pest control strategies you can develop.** Every insect pest, even those that aren't native to the Northeast, has at least one predator or parasite. In a healthy, well-established garden, the balance between pests and their foes keeps insect damage to a tolerable minimum. As you build soils with organic matter and control pests and diseases without harmful chemicals, natural balances will begin to assert themselves in your garden.

119 **Most beneficial insect species require nectars and pollens in the adult phase of their lives**. They also appreciate some shaded areas and shallow pools of water. Set up habitats for these insects in an unobstrusive spot, preferably close to their favorite foods, flowering mints, yarrows, thymes, and annuals such as sweet alyssum and salvia. Set an aluminum pie plate on the soil and change the water every day. A couple of rocks keep it from blowing away and give insects a perch while they're drinking.

120 **Hand-pick as many large insects as you can.** This isn't the most glamorous way to spend Sunday afternoon, but it's certainly the most effective way to get rid of many pests. Pick off large insects such as rose chafers and Japanese beetles. If you don't like crushing them, drop them in a bucket of water to which you've added a teaspoon or so of gasoline. As you search for the adult insects, look for larvae and eggs too. Check a good insect identification book to learn what they look like so you won't kill your allies by mistake. For example, ladybug larvae look like some strange kind of pest and their eggs look like smaller versions of the Colorado potato beetle's.

121 If you have to control an insect with a pesticide, try to use a product made from botanical sources. These materials break down into relatively harmless substances within a day or two, but even so, should be used only as a last resort. Natural pesticides include insecticidal soap, neem, pyrethrin, rotenone, ryania, and sabadilla. Of these, rotenone is the most dangerous to your garden since it kills many beneficial insects along with the pests. It's sometimes a better environmental choice than a synthetic chemical pesticide, but try other materials first.

122 You can outwit cutworms. These beetle larvae live in the soil and emerge at night to eat your seedlings, either by squeezing the stems so tightly that the plant falls over or by crawling up the stems to ravish young leaves. There are several ways to defeat these pests. In a small garden, surround each transplant stem with a cardboard collar. In gardens large enough to make that impractical, try toothpicks. As you transplant, encircle each seedling stem with three to four toothpicks, placed right up against the stem. Toothpick wood is too strong for the cutworm to sever and the points at the top of the toothpicks are sharp enough to discourage crawling.

123 If you're seeing lots of aphids, have your soil tested. Aphids are rarely troublesome in a healthy home garden because ladybugs and tiny parasitic wasps keep them in control. But if you do get an aphid problem, suspect nitrogen excesses. To fix the problem in the current season, spray plants with an insecticidal soap, available from most garden supply shops. If that doesn't work, try spraying with a 1 percent formulation of rotenone, mixed according to label directions. Check the results of the soil test before you add any nitrogen sources the next year.

124 In cool, moist spring and fall weather, start watching for slugs. Great ragged holes in plant leaves are your best clue that the slugs have arrived. If you suspect slug damage, lay old boards on the soil surface, near the plants being attacked. Each morning, lift the boards and pick off the slugs. If you dislike this method, try beer traps. Bury cans or old cups to their rims and fill them with beer every night. Some slugs are sure to crawl in and drown.

125 If you have a large infestation of Japanese beetles, get set to attack them on as many fronts as possible. First, hand-pick as many adults as you can. Next, to kill the beetle larvae in the soil, buy a product containing beneficial nematodes. Milky spore disease, a bacteria that preys on the larvae, is not reliable in cold-season climates such as the Northeast, but you can count on the nematodes. Apply them as directed on the box, taking care to water at least as much, if not more, than recommended. Finally, if there are more beetles than you can possibly hand-pick, set up a Japanese beetle trap. Place the trap as far away from the garden as possible so that beetles lured to it won't stop off for lunch on the way.

126 Start patrolling for rose chafers in early May. Not only do the adults feed on the flowers and leaves of roses (*Rosa* spp.), peonies (*Paeonia* spp.), irises (*Iris* spp.), dahlias (*Dahlia* spp.), and hollyhocks (*Alcea rosea*), the soil-dwelling larvae eat the roots of these plants as well as grasses and weeds. Again, hand-pick as many as possible and then apply beneficial nematodes to the surrounding soil. In serious infestations, spray plants with pyrethrin.

127 Thrips are so tiny that you'll see their damage long before you see them. If your flower buds are dropping before blooming or foliage has silvery speckling or streaking, suspect thrips. Ladybugs and other beneficial insects prey on them but in a large infestation, you may need to take direct action. Spray with insecticidal soap and wait a week. If damage persists, use neem, ryania, or sabadilla on plant leaves.

128 **When you mow the lawn, tarnished plant bugs decide to move into your flower garden.** These pests can be fierce in the Northeast. Vegetable gardeners routinely cover their beds with old sheets or row cover material while they're mowing, but this system is rarely practical for flower gardeners. Instead, watch for tarnished plant bugs on flower buds that are just opening. They seem to prefer yellow and can destroy yellow statice (*Limonium sinuatum*), sunflowers (*Helianthus* spp.), and tickseed (*Coreopsis* spp.). If damage is severe, apply sabadilla just before you mow to kill them before they do much damage.

129 **Begin watching for harlequin bugs in the mid- to late summer when the roadside milkweed they've been eating begins to dry up.** These gaudy red and black insects can suck the sap out of your flowers in only a few days. Watch for them on dahlias

(*Dahlia* spp.) and butterfly weed (*Asclepias tuberosa*), particularly. Pick them off as soon as you see them and monitor your plants every day for new infestations. If they get out of control, spray with pyrethrin.

Avoiding Plant Diseases

130 Plan your flower garden to facilitate the good air circulation that defends against so many fungal diseases. Beds where all the plants are the same height and shape tend to trap moist air. But if adjacent plants are varying sizes and shapes, breezes have an easier time blowing through them.

131 Good watering practices also help to prevent diseases. As much as possible, position plants close to each other that have similar watering requirements. This kind of advance planning will allow you to irrigate the water-hungry plants heavily without overwatering the others.

132 Protect your plants from diseases with good cultural care. The stronger the plant, the more resistant it is to diseases. General preventive tactics include keeping water and nutrient supplies adequate but not excessive and pruning off all old leaves and any fallen fruit. In the fall, compost all the old plant debris and remove stakes, pots, trellises, and so on from the garden area. If you do see a lot of diseases, get your soil tested, since diseases are most likely to attack plants with a nutrient imbalance.

⟨133⟩ When diseases are in your garden, try to protect plants from the insects that spread them. For example, most viruses are spread by aphids and leafhoppers who pick up the virus-infected cell sap as they feed and then inject it into cells of healthy plants. Other insects spread diseases just by walking through a patch of infective bacteria or fungal spores and then tracking it onto new plants. The best controls for these insects are their natural enemies, so it's best to use a pesticide that won't kill them. Additionally, you can also reduce the spread of diseases by picking off and destroying the diseased leaves, stems, and flowers on your plants.

⟨134⟩ Effective controls for diseases include copper, sulfur, lime sulfur, dormant oil, and superior horticultural oil. Since each of these materials has the potential to injure plant tissue while it's killing the disease organism, it's wise to exercise some caution when using them. Read labels carefully and dilute and use materials as directed. If you plan to spray, buy disposable masks at the hardware store. Even though these materials aren't poisons, they can be irritating to your respiratory system.

◇135◇ Researchers are discovering that foliar sprays of compost tea protect plants against many fungal diseases, as long as the sprays are applied before the disease spores land on the plant. Compounds in the tea prevent some fungal spores from germinating and kill others. Make the tea by suspending an old pillowcase filled with several quarts of fully finished compost in a 55-gallon barrel of water. Cover the barrel and let the tea "steep" for 10 to 14 days. Then remove the bag of compost. Protect your sprayer from clogs by straining the tea through a coffee filter before you use it. If the tea looks quite dark, it may be too nutrient-rich. Protect your plants from excesses by diluting the solution until it looks like weak tea. Spray plant leaves with the tea at intervals of every two to three weeks through the season. As with all foliar sprays, it's best to spray on cloudy days or early enough so leaves dry before the sun shines brightly.

136 With advance planning, you can prevent powdery mildew attacks. This fungus disease infects many different flowering plants, particularly perennial phlox (*Phlox* spp.), roses (*Rosa* spp.), and lilacs (*Syringa* spp.), usually in late summer and early fall. But you can prevent most attacks by spraying susceptible plants with compost tea. Begin in late July or early August and dilute the tea more than you would if you were using it as a fertilizer. If this doesn't appeal to you, use a mixture of 1 tablespoon superior horticultural oil and 1 tablespoon baking soda mixed into a gallon of water. Wait to spray this mixture until the first sign of infection.

137 You're most likely to see gray mold, or *Botrytis* spp., on soft-leaved plants such as begonias (*Begonia* spp.), peonies (*Paeonia* spp.), and geraniums (*Pelargonium* spp.). Protect plants by placing them in soils with good drainage where they receive at least six hours a day of good sunlight. Space so air circulates around the leaves. If you've had infections in the past, spray your plants at intervals of 10 to 14 days with compost tea.

138 **You can recognize aster yellows disease by leaves that yellow without spotting, often in combination with dwarfed and distorted flower growth or abnormally erect stems.** This disease attacks many plants in the composite family, including vegetables. Leafhoppers carry aster yellows from one plant to another. Protect your plants by removing any that are diseased. Destroy unhealthy weeds such as wild asters, chicory, dandelions, thistles, and wild carrot (Queen Anne's lace) because they also carry it.

Fall Care

139 **Fall weeding will make your spring work much easier.** Of course, by this time in the year, weeding is the last thing most of us want to do. But for the sake of the coming season, try to make yourself do it. Dig perennial weeds that may have sprouted over the summer and hoe out the tiny rosettes of winter annuals such as shepherd's purse and peppergrass. When you're finished, you'll know that you can look forward to a much tidier garden in the spring.

140 **One of the most important secrets of good gardeners is the attention they give to cleaning up the**

garden in the fall. By cleaning up well, they eliminate many of the overwintering spots for both pests and diseases. Start clean-up as soon as your first annuals die. Pull these plants from the beds and add them to the compost piles. Pick up all the old pots, stakes, and other equipment in the yard. Wash everything and let it dry in the sun before storing it for the winter. Scrape soil from your tools and then coat the metal surfaces with oil before storing.

◆**141**◆ **Mulch to protect perennials from heaving out of the ground during winter thaws.** Deep mulches keep the soil consistently cold, thus preventing the normal contraction/ expansion cycles that uproot so many plants. Although it's tempting to mulch the garden while the weather's still warm, try to resist the impulse. Mulching before the ground freezes can do more harm than good. Wait until the top inch or so of the soil has frozen, generally in early November for the northernmost part of the Northeast and mid- to late November in southern areas.

◆**142**◆ **Use different mulching techniques on different plants.** Deep mulches can rot the crowns of some, particularly during winter thaws.

Avoid covering the crowns of delphiniums (*Delphinium* spp.), irises (*Iris* spp.), oriental poppies (*Papaver* spp.), and peonies (*Paeonia* spp.) unless you are in a windy zone 3 location. When mulching plants that retain green leaves far into the fall such as foxgloves (*Digitalis* spp.), hollyhocks (*Alcea rosea*), and primroses (*Primula* spp.), lay the mulch under the leaves. Never mulch daylilies (*Hemerocallis* spp.); their leaves provide all the mulch they need and they rot if smothered under moist materials.

HOW SHOULD YOUR GARDEN GROW?

Flowers in Containers

143 **Choose appropriately sized pots for container plants.** Look around to see what sizes are generally used for the plants you want to place in containers and follow these examples. If you must make a choice between two sizes, pick the larger. The larger the soil mass in the pot, the better it will retain water.

144 **Container plants need supplementary fertilization.** Each week, feed them with a liquid seaweed and fish emulsion solution. You can buy these ingredients separately or, frequently, find a premixed combination of them. Because you are feeding so often, avoid overfertilizing by using a half-strength dilution. For example, if the directions say to mix 1 tablespoon of the material into a gallon of water, use only half a tablespoon.

145 **Peat moss is a container plant's best friend.** Not only does it help the soil mix to retain water, it can also add needed humidity around plants in high light situations. Pot your plant as usual and then prepare a larger container by adding a layer of peat moss in the bottom. Set the plant pot into the larger container and pack peat moss between the two pots. Each time you water, soak the peat moss too.

146 **Routine maintenance keeps your hanging baskets looking their best through the summer season.** Most basket plants are "under potted," meaning that they don't have adequate root room. As well, the baskets are often in very exposed conditions where the soil dries rapidly. Keep your baskets looking good by fertilizing as suggested above and watering well at least once or preferably twice a day. Pick off old blooms and prune plants as necessary to keep their shape pleasing.

147 **Use small trailing plants such as lobelia (*Lobelia* spp.) in hanging baskets.** Since nurseries charge so much for baskets, it only makes sense to grow your own. Take a tip from the professionals: when you plant the seeds for tiny plants that you'll pot up into baskets, sow five or six seeds in every small pot. When you transplant them into the baskets, use four groups to a pot, placing one in the center and three spaced around the perimeter. In no time at all, the plants will look evenly seeded in the basket.

148 **Growers encourage plants such as cascading petunias (*Petunia* x *hybrida*) and lobelia (*Lobelia* spp.) to drape.** Once you know the trick, it's easy. Let the plants grow as they will until they are 8 to 10 inches tall. From then on, each time you water, spray down into the center of the pot. The water pressure will force the stems outward and over the pot. Voilà, a cascading plant!

Spring Bulbs

149 **If your soil is soggy in the winter and early spring, make a raised bed for your bulbs.** Spring flowering bulbs absolutely require well-drained soil. You don't need to enclose the bed with boards or bricks, but you do need to slope it so that water will naturally drain from it.

150 **Plant your bulbs in wire "bulb cages."** Burrowing rodents sometimes eat bulbs, particularly the tulips, during the winter. But cages foil their attempts. Although you can buy these contraptions from bulb suppliers, it's easy to make your own. Cut chicken wire into 1-foot squares. Put two squares together so that they make a tighter mesh and bend the squares to enclose a bulb. Leave plenty of space between the bulb and the sides of the cage. Roots, leaves, and flower stems can grow through the openings but rodents can't get to the bulb.

151 **Use gravity, mixed with common sense, to create an area where bulbs are naturalized.** As generally advised, toss the bulbs into the air and let them land where they will. But don't plant them exactly where they fell. Since you want to be able to leave them in place over a few years to multiply and be a carefree garden, you're better off rearranging them somewhat. Leave at least eight inches between each bulb and its neighbor.

152 Don't let your lawn mower destroy the naturalized bulb planting. Long after they've finished blooming, bulb plants are still busy making sugars to store for the following year. If you cut off their leaves before they naturally brown and dry, you'll be limiting their food reserves. This may kill them outright or simply prevent them from blooming the following year. If grasses get out of control before the bulbs' foliage dies back, use hand clippers to cut it.

153 Hide dying bulb leaves with freshly growing leaves and flowers of other plants. Interplant your bulb bed with plants such as winter-hardy pansies (*Viola* x *Wittrockiana*), violas (*Viola tricolor*), or forget-me-nots (*Myosotis palustris*). These plants bloom so early and fill in bed areas so quickly that you'll hardly notice the old daffodil or tulip leaves.

Wildflowers

◈ **154** **Newly-seeded wildflowers do not compete well with weeds.** To help them along, prepare their site by digging out the roots of perennial weeds and then tilling or pulling annual weeds. Keep the area weeded through the first season so that the planting can eventually take care of itself. If you can't tell the wildflowers' seed leaves–the germinating plant's first leaves–from those of the weeds, plant some of your wildflower mix in a flat or big pot. You'll soon learn to recognize their seed leaves.

◈ **155** **Wildflower patches look best when plants are evenly distributed through the area.** When planting a large wildflower patch, it's sometimes hard to spread seed uniformly. The most reliable method is to divide the site into equal sections. Divide your seeds evenly into the same number of envelopes, making certain that some of each kind is in each batch. Then use one envelope to plant each section.

◈ **156** **Wildflower plantings change over the years.** The largest, most aggressive plants usually begin to crowd out the more dainty species. You can let this process occur as it does in nature. Or, if you miss the more delicate plants, thin out the aggressors every spring. Similarly, if blooms begin to diminish in size or number, thin the plants so they aren't overcrowded.

Annuals

157 **Annual flowers are a must.** Whatever your garden design, you can find an annual with just the right color, size, and texture for it. Most annuals are fast to bloom, so you can have an "instant" garden. With proper care, many annuals flower from early summer till frost. To extend the bloom time of the few short-season annuals, make successive plantings through the early part of the season.

158 **"Deadheading," or removing spent blooms before seeds mature, keeps most annual plants productive through the season.** Develop the habit of cutting or pinching off faded flowers as you stroll through the garden. When you're pressed for time, doing this every fourth or fifth day generally extends bloom times.

159 **Let some annuals self-seed.** To encourage them, leave a few faded blossoms on selected plants, starting in the middle of their season. The following spring, you can transplant some of the "volunteers" to new spots in the garden or simply thin and leave them where they're growing. To protect against pests and diseases that build up when the same plants grow in the same places, try to move your volunteers around after two years.

160 **Stretch your seed budget by saving seed from your favorite non-hybrid plants**. (Hybrid plants have parents of at least two different species and are labeled as "hybrid" or "F_1" or "F_2" on the seed packet.) To save good seed, let the seedpods or flower heads mature on the plant. When they begin to dry, watch them daily. You'll want to collect the seeds before they drop to the soil. After collecting, let the seeds continue drying. Set them in open glass jars and pour them from one jar to another every day. After a week or so, package them, labeled, in small plastic bags with closable seals and store the bags in a closed container in the refrigerator. Some seeds, such as delphinium, must freeze before they'll germinate. When in doubt about their freezing requirements, store half the seeds in the freezer and half in the refrigerator.

161 Plants grown from seed produced by hybrids sometimes revert to a parental form, often smaller and with different coloration than the plant you grew. If you want the original, buy fresh seed every year. However, it's fun to see what grows from self-saved seed of hybrids. Pansies (*Viola* x *Wittrockiana*), petunias (*Petunia* x *hybrida*), annual poppies (*Papaver* spp.), and sunflowers (*Helianthus* spp.) are only a few of the hybrid species that produce interesting children.

Biennials

162 Plant some biennials to find out why they're worth the wait. These plants take two years to complete their growth cycle, growing only leaves the first season and flowers the second. Try growing larkspur (*Consolida ambigua*), canterbury bells (*Campanula medium*), hollyhocks (*Alcea rosea*), foxgloves (*Digitalis* spp.), money plants (*Lunaria annua*), and sweet William (*Dianthus barbatus*).

163 Save time and space by waiting to set out biennials until midsummer. Plan to replace an early-flowering annual with a biennial. Start these plants in flats or pots in early to mid-June and then transplant them into the garden in mid- to late July. This timing allows them to establish themselves well enough for a glorious bloom the following year.

164 **Use the spectacular foliage of some biennials as a focal point or background in the flower bed.** Hollyhocks (*Alcea rosea*) and money plants (*Lunaria annua*) both have large, crinkly, deep-green leaves that can stand as a background for smaller plants. Sweet Williams (*Dianthus barbatus*) make a nice combination with lilies (*Lilum* spp.), while larkspur (*Consolida ambigua*) is so delicate that it can be woven in and out of any perennial bed.

Perennials

165 **Keep an eye on the invasive perennials.** These plants try to take over the garden, either by sneaking their roots into other plantings or spreading their seeds far and wide. Although this can seem a benefit when you're trying to fill in a border or build planting stock, it can also be a nuisance. There are two solutions to this problem. In the case of plants that self-seed, you'll need to weed out the extra plants every spring. Plants that spread from roots can be dug out every year or, if you tire of this, grown in pots. If you want the plants to look as if they're growing in the bed, dig holes and sink the pots, covering their rims with about an inch of soil or mulching material.

166 **Don't be afraid to move your plants around.** Perennial gardens rarely turn out exactly right the first time you plant them. More often than not, what looked like a good color combination on paper turns out to be disastrous, or a plant grows a foot higher than you expected. To keep your design pleasing, you'll have to move the offending plant. Fall transplanting is often advised. But in the Northeast, it's much safer to do this work in the early spring, just as the plant begins to break its winter dormancy. If you must divide plants in the fall, time it so that the roots have at least a month to establish themselves before the soil gets cold.

167 **Vigorous, quickly growing perennials outgrow the space allotted to them every few years.** To keep these plants healthy, you'll need to divide them. As a general rule, plan to do this every third or fourth year. In spring, lift the plants with a spading fork. Now pull, pry, or cut the root mass into two or three sections. Replant these divisions at the same depth they were growing. If you can't use them all, pot them up and give them to friends and neighbors.

168 Grow some long-blooming perennials amongst your shorter-season favorites. Not only will you enjoy these flowers for a longer time each year, you'll also appreciate the way they "anchor" your perennial beds. Choose from yarrow (*Achillea* spp.), astilbe (*Astilbe* x *arendsii*), tickseed (*Coreopsis* spp.), blanket flower (*Gaillardia*), coral bells (*Heuchera*), sundrops (*Oenothera* spp.), false dragonhead (*Physostegia*), black-eyed Susan (*Rudbeckia* spp.), speedwell (*Veronica* spp.), and pansies (*Viola* x *Wittrockiana*).

Cutting Gardens

169 Plant your cutting garden for utility, not for looks. Set out your plants as if they were vegetables, in easy-to-care-for rows and beds. This system will allow you to concentrate on the appropriate nutrition, light exposure, and care of each plant. As well, cutting will be faster and you'll always be conscious of which plants are coming into bloom and which need deadheading.

170 **Plan to cut from both annuals and perennials.** Since you'll probably want to make as many mixed bouquets as single-species arrangements, it's best to have a variety of plants in bloom through the season. To plan for this, make a list of all the perennials you grow, noting bloom times. Now think of annuals that both complement the forms and colors of the perennials and also bloom at the correct time. If you ever have a gap, make a note of the timing and use an annual to cover for it the following year.

171 **Newly cut flowers can wilt faster than a leaf of lettuce on a sidewalk in August.** Prevent wilting by cutting in the morning, just after the dew has dried. If you can't get to it then, wait until twilight, just before the dew falls. Always carry a bucket, half-filled with cool water, into the garden. As you snip each stem, immediately put it in the bucket.

172 **For longest vase life, "condition" your flowers.** After cutting, bring the bucket of flowers inside, to the coolest, darkest area available. Fill a second bucket with 6 inches of cool water. Take each stem from the first bucket, strip leaves from the lower third to half the stem, and move it to the second bucket. With your hands and the stem under water, recut, generally at an angle. Do this to each of the stems in turn. Now leave them immersed in the water for 2 to 3 hours before moving them to the vase where you'll arrange them.

◆173◆ **Burn stems that exude a milky sap.** This sap clogs the vessels, preventing the flowers from taking up new water supplies. Poppies (*Papaver* spp.), zinnias (*Zinnia* spp.), and snow-on-the-mountain (*Euphorbia marginata*) all do this. But you can prolong their vase life if you singe their stems. When you go into the garden, take both your water bucket and long kitchen matches. As you cut each stem, hold it over the flame until it's singed. Now set it in the water bucket. Let these stems sit in a cool, dark place for several hours before you arrange them.

◆174◆ **Make your own flower preservative.** Commercial preservatives contain sugar, mildly acidifying ingredients, and an agent to kill bacteria. While these solutions are the easiest to use, many growers have discovered that a homemade concoction works just as well. And the recipe's a snap: add 2 to 3 tablespoons of sugar and a capful of laundry bleach to 5 gallons of water.

VINES AND SHRUBS

❀ ❀ ❀

175 **Invest in some clematis (*Clematis* spp.).** These vines are one of the easiest and most spectacular of all garden perennials. Because they are equally happy twining around a free-standing trellis, climbing strings against a wall, or growing through a large rosebush, they are adaptable to almost any garden design. Plant them in deep, moderately-rich soils. To perform at their best, they like their top growth exposed to sunlight and their roots cool, so deep mulches around them not only bring out their looks, they also keep them healthy. Incidentally, while many clematis grow best in zones 5 and 6, *C. jackmanii* survives in almost all locations in zone 4 and protected areas in zone 3.

176 If you garden in horticultural zones 3 and 4, you may have to work to keep perennial vines alive through the long cold winters. Begin by looking at area yards to see what other gardeners are growing. Ask about the particular cultivar, of course, but also look at the plant's location. The best way to keep many of these plants alive is by protecting them from the cold winter winds, either by planting in a walled garden or using a hedgerow of conifers to shield them from prevailing winds.

177 If you have trouble keeping perennials alive through your cold winters, try growing annuals instead. Even in zone 3, they're always reliable. For best results, start your seeds inside, planting into 3- to 4-inch peat pots. Since most of these vines are tender annuals, you should plant them about 5 to 6 weeks before your frost-free date. Transplant them outside once you're certain that the frosts are over and enjoy their flowers, fragrances, and the shade they can give to a west-facing porch.

178 Lilacs (*Syringa* spp.) grow well in all areas of the Northeast, with *S. villosa*, or late lilac, and *S. vulgaris*, or common lilac, being the most

reliably hardy in cold, windy, zone 3 conditions. Though easy to grow, lilacs always stay healthier if you plant them in well-drained soil that has a pH close to 7. If your soil is acid, add a cup of bonemeal to the hole when you plant and remember to sprinkle a handful around the base of the plant each fall. Increase your blooms by pruning off spent flowers before they make seeds each year and protect against powdery mildew as directed in tip 136.

179 **Hydrangeas (*Hydrangea* spp.) are an almost totally carefree shrub as long as they have adequate water.** They can also tell you about the pH of your soil. In acid conditions, blooms are blue, while in alkaline soils, they're pink. You can change a blue bush to a pink one by adding lime to the soil and a pink bush to a blue one by mulching with acid-containing materials such as peat moss or wood chips.

180 **Peonies (*Paeonia* spp.) are not only easy to grow, they live for decades, gradually enlarging each year by forming new "eyes," or growing buds, on their ever-expanding crowns.** Old plants can be as much as 4 or 5 feet in diameter. This steady growth requires good humus and fertility. Every spring, apply ½ to 1 inch of compost from the base of the plant to slightly beyond its drip line. Peonies don't need dividing more than once every dozen or so years, but you can take divisions to enlarge your bed. In early September, dig the peony clump with a spading fork. Using a sharp knife, cut the roots into divisions containing no less than three eyes each. Replant these in compost-amended soil, burying the eyes no more than 2 to 3 inches deep. Mulch the plants over the winter and uncover them in early spring when the new buds peek out of the soil.

181 **Butterfly bushes (*Buddleia* spp.) are gratifying shrubs, particularly in late summer when, it's true, butterflies flock to drink the nectar.** In much of the Northeast, the top growth dies back every winter. However, once spring weather arrives, growth resumes. By late August, second-year and older plants reach their full height of 5 feet. These bushes are a snap to maintain. Plant them in deep, moderately rich, well-drained soil. Keep them mulched through the summer. If the top growth dies over winter, cut it back in March, while the plant is still dormant.

TIPS FOR
SUCCESS
WITH
SPECIFIC
PLANTS

182 **Thrift (*Armeria* spp.) is a lovely plant for the edge of the border, particularly since it keeps a dark green color through the year.** The ball-shaped flowers of pink, rose, mauve, and deep red have long wiry stems and hold for as long as 10 days in the vase. This perennial is easy to start from seed. Soak the seed for 48 hours before planting and keep the starting flats at 70°F. Seeds will germinate within 2 weeks.

Transplant the seedlings to the garden about 2 weeks before the last frost.

183 Since it's so hard to choose between perennial asters (*Aster* spp.) and the annuals we call asters (*Callistephus chinensis*), grow both. But no matter which you choose, rotate their positions in the garden. Move annuals every year and perennials every 2 to 4 years. Annual asters are vulnerable to a disease called aster yellows, but if you keep moving them around, you'll probably never see it. Fungus diseases, particularly wilts and mildews, attack the perennial species, especially those in crowded conditions. By lifting, dividing, and rotating these plants, you can keep them spaced widely enough apart to discourage these diseases.

184 Baby's breath (*Gypsophila* spp.), whether perennial or annual, is a carefree plant. The perennial, with its tiny flowers, adds lightness to a garden border and can also be air-dried for use in winter arrangements. Annual baby's breath has larger flowers and is lovely in the garden and as a "filler" in arrangements. Start perennial baby's breath inside, about 8 weeks before your frost-free date. It's cold-hardy enough to take light frosts, but don't tempt fate by planting it more than two weeks before the weather has settled. Annuals can be started inside 6 weeks before the frost-free date. For bloom through the season, seed it in the garden in early June, early July, and early August.

185 **Plant cold-hardy calendula (*Calendula officinalis*) for blooms from late June until very heavy frost.** This annual is easy to grow, whether seeded directly in the garden or started early indoors. Darkness increases its germination rate, so cover direct-seeded crops with ¼-inch of soil. If you're starting seeds in flats or pots, lay a piece of heavy cardboard or a section or two of newspaper over them for the 10 days the plants take to germinate. Pick off spent flowers to keep the plants blooming through the season.

186 **Candytuft (*Iberis* spp.), whether annual or perennial, has the purest of all white flowers in the garden.** Other colors are available too, but grow at least a few of the white forms to use in bouquets or as a fine edging plant. Annual candytufts (*Iberis* spp.) are easy to grow and bloom so quickly that a direct seeding in early spring can give you flowers through the season. Perennial forms grow readily but do not overwinter well unless they are planted in well-drained soil in a location where they receive midday shade, even during the dark days of winter.

◈ **187** **Chrysanthemums (*Chrysanthemum* spp.) are among the easiest plants to lift and move from one location to another.** This quality makes them an ideal landscaping plant. For example, you can grow a row of cushion mums in the vegetable garden all summer and then transplant them, in late August or early September, to a border near the door. These transplanted mums will bloom as if they'd never been disturbed.

◈ **188** **Plant cosmos (*Cosmos* spp.) in the right soil and you'll have blooms from early summer until frost.** This plant prefers well-drained soil that hasn't seen compost or other fertilizers for two years or so. In nutrient-rich spots, cosmos will make rank growth and have few to no flowers until late summer. This plant definitely rates as one of the best self-seeders. If you let it go to seed, expect a huge patch of new cosmos the following year.

189 Crepis (*Crepis rubra*) deserves wider attention and more frequent planting than it gets. This relatively unknown annual produces lovely pink composite flowers on 12-inch stems. The flowers cut well and also make a bright splash of color in the mid- to late-season border. Like cosmos, crepis grows best in lean, well-drained soils, tolerating conditions dry enough to wilt many another plant.

190 Stately delphiniums (*Delphinium* spp.) belong in every garden. Not only are the tall spikes of flowers lovely, the deeply serrated and mounded foliage adds a touch of elegance. As a Northeastern gardener, you can expect it to thrive. Our cool summers and high humidity levels bring out the best in both color and size. But you must also be prepared to stake the flower spikes to keep them upright. Green 6-foot-tall bamboo stakes and green twistee-ties are the least obtrusive staking method.

191 Lace flowers (*Trachelium caeruleum*) are ideal annuals for the Northeast since their preferred climate is just what the region offers—cool summer temperatures and high humidity levels. The plants grow to about 30 inches tall, producing sprays of delicate, lacelike flowers of either white or blue. Start plants inside, about 6 weeks before the frost-free date, transplant after that date, and sit back and watch the show, or cut for arrangements, all summer long.

192 **Tassel flowers (*Emilia javanica, E. flammea*) produce more blooms in a season than you can imagine, much less cut.** The small (½-inch wide) scarlet to orange fuzzy balls grow on stems 12 to 15 inches long. In the border, they add an airy touch of brightness. In arrangements, they can be used as fillers or, when paired with a larger, less complicated bloom such as a white cosmos or a Shasta daisy, the main show. These annuals are easy to grow and will produce as well in hot humid conditions as they do in cooler weather. Since it's so hard to keep up with the flowers from this plant, expect some self-seeded volunteers in following seasons.

193 **Try godetia (*Godetia* spp.).** Their common name is satin flower, no doubt in honor of their petals' high, smooth sheen. These annuals are graceful in the garden and spectacular in arrangements. If their good looks aren't enough to whet your interest, their 2-week vase-life should convince you to grow them. But there is one disadvantage to godetia—they are sure to attract Japanese beetles. Be prepared. In early summer, hang Japanese beetle traps as far away from the garden as possible. As soon as the weather warms, begin patrolling too, looking for stray beetles that you can pick off the plants. This care will be amply repaid by some of the prettiest flowers you've ever seen.

194 **Gladiolus (*Gladiolus* spp.) are almost carefree in the Northeastern climate as long as you take a few reasonable precautions.** Buy solid, healthy corms, ideally from a garden supply store where you can pick and choose among them. Plant them, after the frost-free date, 4 to 5 inches deep and anywhere from 6 to 8 inches apart. For a longer bloom time, plant a second batch of corms two weeks later. Keep the plants well watered since moisture stress can prevent blooming. Stake, using thin bamboo sticks, as soon as the flower spike begins to develop. Cut them when the bottom two flowers are open.

195 **Lavatera (*Lavatera trimestris*) makes a grand display in Northeastern gardens.** These 2½- to 3-foot tall, bushy annuals have dark-green, glossy leaves. Starting in midsummer and continuing till frost, white or pink 3- to 4-inch wide flowers cover the plant. Lavatera flowers resemble old-fashioned single hollyhocks. Start lavatera seeds inside 6 weeks before the frost-free date or seed directly in the garden in late May. Plant them in well-drained soils and keep them a little on the dry side. When you cut them, take whole stems just as the first flowers begin to open.

196 **Pansies (*Viola* x *Wittrockiana*) usually bloom for the entire season in the Northeast, making them one of the best gardening bargains available.** You can buy seed each year and start your plants early (10 weeks before the frost-free date) or buy started plants from a garden supply store. To prolong the bloom season, pinch off spent blossoms until late July. After that, let a few seedpods form and ripen. The following spring, look carefully for the plants these seeds produced and thin them out or transplant some to a new bed. Even though these pansies won't be the same as their hybrid parents, you'll probably get some unexpected colors that you love.

197 **Purple coneflowers (*Echinacea purpurea*) were once uncommon in the Northeast but are**

becoming more and more popular as gardeners discover how easy they are to grow and how spectacular a display they make. Though you can buy plants, it's less expensive to start your own. You'll need to stratify these seeds by placing the seed packet in the refrigerator for 4 weeks. Afterwards, plant them in furrows in a starting flat and cover the seeds with vermiculite to let light penetrate. Germination will occur in 15 to 20 days. Leave 2 feet between the plants when you set them into the garden. Divide the roots every 3 years to keep the plants healthy.

◇198◇ **Both annual and perennial scabiosa (*Scabiosa* spp.) cultivars make excellent plants for the ornamental flower garden.** Though both can be used as cut flowers, the annuals produce more steadily through the season. Similar to so many other cut-flower species, scabiosa performs at its very best in our Northeastern summers with their cool nights and long days. Start seeds of perennial scabiosa about 10 weeks before the frost-free date and annual scabiosa about 6 weeks before then. Even though the plants have some frost tolerance, it's best to wait until the weather's reliably warm before setting them out. Place them in full sun, leaving 24 inches between perennials and 10 to 15 inches between annuals. Cut them when the flowers are almost completely open. They last at least a week in the vase.

199 Both annual and perennial statice (*Limonium* spp.) can be used in fresh arrangements or dried for winter bouquets. Annual statice (*Limonium sinuatum*) is easy to grow in almost any environment. However, if you're interested in maximum production of very long stems, take a tip from commercial growers. Plant the annual seed in shallow furrows in the flat and cover it with vermiculite. After it germinates in 1 to 2 weeks, wait until the seed leaves have fully expanded and then move it to a location where temperatures range between 50 and 55°F. Keep it in this spot for 5 to 8 weeks, or until it has five leaves. Transplant it to the garden once the threat of serious frost has passed.

200 Sunflowers (*Helianthus* spp.) are no longer confined to great big yellow blooms with dark centers. If you look in any seed catalogue these days, you'll see that breeders have developed cultivars with double flowers, dwarf sizes, and colors ranging from white to deep mahogany. If you decide to grow some of these beauties, remember to plant them after the last frost in soil with high fertility levels. Keep them watered through the season. If you don't pick them all, be prepared for some surprising volunteers the following year. Even though your second year plants won't all have the characteristics of their parents, they're also sure to be beautiful.

INDEX

Please note: the numbers below refer to the tips, not the book's pages.